KidCaps' Presents

Jamestown
A History Just for Kids

KidCaps is An Imprint of BookCaps™
www.bookcaps.com

Table of Contents

About KidCaps

KidCaps is an imprint of BookCaps™ that is just for kids! Each month BookCaps will be releasing several books in this exciting imprint. Visit are website or like us on Facebook to see more!

Introduction

The weather is starting to get very cold. It is December of 1607, and Captain John Smith is one of the men who are in charge of the Jamestown colony. Things are not going well. They have been in America for about eight months, and winter is almost here. Even so, they have hardly any food, their living conditions are poor, and they did not have time to plant any crops in the time since they arrived.

Things have gotten so bad that Captain John Smith has been sent to explore the Chickahominy River to try to find something for the large group of colonists to eat. But it's not easy; after all, there are over 40 hungry men back at the fort, waiting for him to bring them food.

There used to be 104 of them.

Captain John Smith feels a huge weight on his shoulders. A lot of the men, who had come from England to colonize the "New World" (as they were calling America) weren't prepared at all for the hard life that they would have to lead here. They weren't prepared to cut down trees for wood, to hunt for their food, to farm the land, and to bring fresh water long distances to their camp. Many of them had already died.

As Captain John Smith explores the river, he is not aware of the Native American warriors, forming part of the Powhatan Confederation, who are hunting nearby. When he stumbles across their path, he knows that he is outnumbered. The fight is brief, and Captain John Smith is captured as a prisoner of war. He is taken a few miles away to the village of Werowocomoco, where he meets the Chief Powhatan

(named *Wahunsenacawh*, he is leader of the local confederation of Native American tribes). Not being able to understand the Algonquin language, Smith doesn't know what is happening. He becomes very afraid, however, when he is forced to place his head on a rock, and it looks like many members of the Powhatan tribe are raising their clubs high up in order to smash Smith's head like a pumpkin. What happened next?

Maybe you have seen this part in a movie. The daughter of Chief Powhatan, Pocahontas, rushes over and flings herself over Smith, and the order is giver to spare his life. Let's listen to the story in Captain John Smith's own words:

> "...at the minute of my execution, she [Pocahontas] hazarded the beating out of her own brains to save mine; and not only that, but so prevailed with her father, that I was safely conducted to Jamestown."

Wow! What an exciting story! Captain John Smith and Pocahontas were two people brought together around the city that Smith came to call home: Jamestown. Where was this city? Why was it built, and who built it? What happened to the first people who lived there, and why is it so important today, over four hundred years later? In this handbook, we are going to take a look at the answers to these questions. Let's start with a brief overview.

Jamestown was originally a fort, and then later a

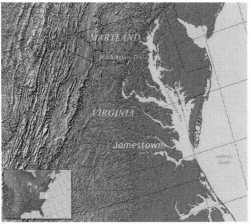

small town, built on the eastern coast of Virginia.

It was the first permanent English settlement in the New World, and was the town where English colonists really got put to the test. It wasn't easy to live in Jamestown. As we will see, the original colonists, and those who joined them in later years, had to contend with lots of different kinds of problems. They had to worry about hostile Native Americans who didn't want white people nearby. They had to contend with fellow colonists who didn't want to work and who just wanted to boss everyone around. They had to try to make a home in a land that wasn't at all like what they were used to.

In short, they had to get the New World ready for the thousands and thousands of people who would come after them.

As we read their story, try to think about what it was like to arrive in a strange place, and to try to make it your new home. Try to think about how you would have fought against the people who wanted to hurt you, how you would have dealt with the lazy colonists, and how you would have found food for your family. You will probably start to see that those who built Jamestown from nothing were just normal people who became real heroes, people who did what was needed, when it was needed. They made a lot of mistakes, because they weren't perfect. But we can still learn a lot from their experiences. Let's read their story.

Chapter 1: What Led Up to the Jamestown settlement?

When Christopher Columbus sailed into the Caribbean Sea in 1492, he changed the course of history forever. His ships, and many ships after him, returned with gold, silver, wood, and slaves from the islands. While explorers and scientists thought about the knowledge that they could acquire and adventures that they could have, and religious leaders thought about expanding their churches to the New World, businessmen and politicians thought about one thing: money.

One European country after another began to send shipload after shipload of colonists to different areas of the New World. Spain decided to keep a few islands in the Caribbean and to colonize most of Central and South America. Portugal focused on what is now called Brazil. The Netherlands, France, Denmark, and even Sweden all rushed to take advantage of these new lands. The English were among the last to take New World conquest seriously.

This is surprising, because it was an explorer sent out

from England, John Cabot, who is generally considered to be the first European since the Vikings to step onto the American continent.

Because the King of England (Henry VII) was busy fighting a war (the Second Cornish Uprising of 1497) he didn't pay a whole lot of attention to the new lands. In fact, he and his successors were more interested in making sure they were making money with business and trade in Europe. So, while Spain, Portugal, and other nations were moving into the New World, England was falling behind. As a result, they could only get very minor footholds in the Caribbean, relying more on "pirates" like Francis Drake to help them get their hands on some of the New World's riches.

All that changed when, in August 1583, under the reign of England's Queen Elizabeth, explorer Humphrey Gilbert successfully sailed to and from North America (specifically, Newfoundland). With his successful return, the English decided that it was time to take colonization of the New World seriously. In fact, several famous writers of that time, like Richard Hakluyt and John Dee, began to get the people in general excited about going to this unexplored land.

On 25 March, 1584, Queen Elizabeth I approved a group of people to be sent to the New World to establish a new colony. They landed on Roanoke. Virginia, and began to build a settlement on August 17, 1585. Things were pretty rough; there were a lot of problems with the local Native Americans, which led to an attack on the colonist's fort. An English Captain had promised to bring them supplies, but the help never came. When Captain Francis Drake went sailing by a little later on his way to England, everyone decided to hop on board and get a ride back to England. The relief eventually came, and the Captain was surprised to find a bunch of empty houses. He left a few men behind. In July of 1587, a large group of colonists arrived to pick them up- and there was no one there. In fact, all they found of the ones who had been left behind was a skeleton on the ground, but they did not know who it had belonged to.

The Captain of this new group of colonist, names Simon Fernandez, forced all of the passengers to get off at Roanoke (even though they were on their way to Chesapeake Bay). The colonists tried to establish friendly relations with the local Native Americans, but the poor treatment that these had received from earlier colonists made it impossible. In fact, one of the colonists, named George Howe, was even killed by a member of a nearby tribe while he was alone on the beach looking for crabs to eat.

The colonists of Roanoke were very afraid. They insisted that their governor, John White, return at once to England to tell the king all about the problems that they were having and to ask for help. He left, but was unable to return for about three years because of England's war with Spain. When he finally returned, he found that all of the colonists, 115 men, women, and children, had completely disappeared. There was no trace of them. To this day, no one is one hundred percent sure what happened.

The first attempt at settling the New World had been a failure.

England decided to try again. This time, the new king of England (James I) allowed private parties to help fund the trip, as a sort of business. Although each colonist had their own reasons for leaving England (some because of religious opposition, others for a desire for adventure, etc…) those who invested money together with the king did so to make money. They formed The Charter of the Virginia Company of London (also known as the London Company).

With this new company, the investors needed a brave man who would be able to help establish the colonists. Who did they choose? His name was Captain John Smith. Of all of the men available, why did the King and his fellow investors choose John Smith for such an important mission?

John Smith, born in 1580 in England, was a natural adventurer. At the age of sixteen, he left England to sail the world and to wander Europe. He ended

becoming what's called a mercenary. Do you know what a mercenary is? A mercenary is basically a "soldier for hire", or a soldier who doesn't fight for just one army. As a mercenary, John Smith fought with the French, the Dutch, the Germans, and was even a pirate for a time in the Mediterranean Sea. He was captured by Ottoman Turks and sold as a slave, but he later escaped and made his way back to England. John Smith was a man who knew how to handle himself in difficult situations and who knew how to be a leader.

The London Company thought that he could be very important to help get their new colony in Virginia established. Do you agree?

In late 1606, three ships named *Susan Constant, Discovery, and Godspeed*, left England for the New World. They stopped off briefly at Puerto Rico, and finally arrived in Virginia on April 26, 1607. About 100 colonists would stay to call the place home.

The founding members of the Jamestown Settlement had arrived.

Chapter 2: Why Did They Settle in Jamestown?

After having read this far, you might have a few questions about the Jamestown settlement. For example, if it was so hard to grow food, why did they choose that area? If the Native Americans were being so hostile, why didn't they move farther away from them? And why was it so difficult to start a colony anyway? Let's learn the answers to these questions.

First, why did the colonists choose an area that made it hard to grow food? Remember that the colonists arrived in the New World late in the month of April, although they didn't even decide where to build their fort until May 14. By that time, it was too late to start planting crops, and the area was really swampy and covered with marshes anyway.

What's more, there was not a lot of fresh water nearby. What they did have was, thanks to the nearby Chesapeake Bay, a whole lot of brackish water (a mixture of salty ocean water and fresh river water). As you might know, brackish water is terrible for plants. Instead of helping them, it can actually do more harm than good.

So why did the colonists choose this area to build their new settlement? The first reason had to do with defense. Remember, during this time, the Spanish and the English were actively fighting against each other. The English would hire men who (like pirates) would attack Spanish ships full of gold and then give the

money to their King. Spain, who was well established in the New World, would not only fight back against the pirates, but also didn't really like the idea of the English trying to get a foothold in the Americas. So the colonists were, more than anything, thinking about how to survive an attack (especially from a Spanish warship). In that situation, the area that became Jamestown was perfect. How so?

Well, the deep water of the Chesapeake would allow the colonists to dock their ships close to the fort, and the way that the land (which was a peninsula) stuck out into the water meant that they could see for a long distance in either direction, and that there would be no sneak attacks from a Spanish warship. Those were some pretty important details for the colonists who were scared of being attacked. However, as we saw, there were more bad things than good things about the location they chose.

The second thing that we wanted to know was: why didn't the colonists just move away from the Native Americans who were giving them so much trouble? Well, the short answer is that their relationship with the Native Americans changed during the years. Let's start with the basics.

The Native American people that lived in the area of Eastern Virginia were part of the Powhatan Confederation. They were originally about 30 tribes, but they decided to join together and to help each other. Each tribe had a local chief (called a *weroance*) but they all recognized the main person in charge, called a Paramount Chief (a *mamanatowick*). When

the colonists arrived, the Paramount Chief was Pocahontas' father, and his name, as we saw in the introduction, was *Wahunsunacawh* (but the English just called him Chief Powhatan).

The colonists arrived, and they soon realized that were going to have to get some food, and quickly. As they were exploring the area that they would eventually call Jamestown, they met the local tribe (called the Paspahegh) and enjoy a delicious feast with them. The experience was so nice that the English decided to build their new fort on Paspahegh land. After all, they were going to need all the friends that they could get in this unexplored land.

As time went on, the Paspahegh began to worry about the colonists. About three weeks later, as they saw that they colonists are not simply travelers passing through, but persons who intend to stay permanently on their lands, a group of about 400 warriors from the Powhatan Confederacy, include some Paspahegh, attacked Jamestown fort, resulting in about four deaths between the two sides. For the next couple of weeks, and the colonists hurried to finish their fort, the Natives made several more raids, and kept trying to get the English to leave. A few weeks later, Paramount Chief *Wahunsunacawh* called for a cease fire. The local Paspahegh respected the decision, and even tried to start helping the colonists again, like the time when they returned a lost English boy to the settlement. On several occasions, they even sold the colonists small amounts of corn so that they wouldn't starve to death.

However, despite the fact that there was no more fighting, tensions kept growing between the two groups- the English colonists and the Native Americans. When John Smith was captured in December of that year (as we read in the introduction), the Paramount Chief asked him and the colonists to move to a different area to establish themselves. When they refused, the relationship got worse and worse, as we will see.

Finally, there is one more question: why was it so hard for the colonists to get things going? Remember, the colonists were starting practically from zero. There were no hardware stores to visit, no internet shopping, no grocery stores. If they wanted food, they had to grow it or hunt it. If they wanted a house, they had to cut down a tree, process the wood, and build it themselves. If they wanted a bathroom, they had to dig a hole in the ground themselves. And if they wanted fresh water for drinking, cooking, or bathing, they had to walk to the river with a bucket and get it.

A lot of the people came to the New World with a spirit of adventure, and they were ready to work. As Captain John Smith later wrote when speaking about the New World:

> "Here every man may be master and owner of his owne labour and land...If he have nothing but his hands, he may...by industrie quickly grow rich."

Of course, we might say that a little differently today. Basically, Smith was saying that anyone, no matter who he is, can become a rich and important person *if he is willing to work.* Coming from a place like England, where a lot of people only care about what family you were born into, that meant that the New World would be a place for a fresh start.

However, not everyone went to the New World ready to work. The London Company, who financed the trip to Virginia, was mostly interested in seeing a return on their investment. In other words, they wanted the Jamestown settlement to find a way of establishing business and to turn a profit. With that in mind, a lot of young businessmen and aristocrats (members of the upper class) found their way onto the three boats that eventually landed in Jamestown. But what do you think? Do you think that these rich businessmen and aristocrats, men who had grown up in houses with servants back in London, were ready to cut down trees for their house, to dig a hole for their toilet, or to plant crops? Of course not! They expected *others* to do all the hard work. In fact, of the hundred or so men and boys that started Jamestown, 47 of them listed "gentleman" as their only job skill! Do you think that being a "gentleman" is a good job skill to start a colony?

So now that we understand a little about the challenges that the Jamestown colonists were facing (difficult growing conditions, hostile Native Americans, and unskilled workers) let's find out exactly what happened after they established themselves and finished building their fort.

Chapter 3: What Happened at the Jamestown Settlement?

As we saw, Jamestown was established in May of 1607. It would eventually become the capital of the young Virginia Colony. It remained the capital until 1699, when there was a fire and the capitol building was rebuilt in nearby Williamsburg. By about the 1750s, the area was abandoned, used mainly for agriculture.

During its history, this first settlement tested the spirit and the character of the original American colonists. Even though many had come to get a fresh start, to have an adventure, or to strike it rich, they had to contend with some serious problems. In this section, let's find out how two of these problems were finally resolved.

Problem #1: Conflicts with Native Americans

Problem #2: Problems with leadership

Let's have a look at each of these to see what happened, and how the colonists reacted.

Problem #1: Conflicts with Native Americans

As we saw previously, the Jamestown colonists seemed to be in constant conflict with the local Paspahegh tribe as well as the larger Powhatan Confederation. During May-December of 1607, they year that the colonists arrived, there were several attacks and even a few deaths. However, after the Paramount Chief ordered a stop to the attacks, the Paspahegh became more peaceable.

When Captain John Smith was captured in December, the Paramount Chief wanted them to leave the Jamestown Area. He suggested that they move to a local village, where they could receive food in exchange for metal tools that they would make for the Natives. John Smith, who had convinced the Chief that he was a very important man and a negotiator for his people, lied and said that he agreed.

During that winter, things got very difficult. The colonists had no food stored up for themselves. Pocahontas' father, *Wahunsunacock* (Chief

Powhatan) gave them corn during the winter, but got really worried when he saw the English practicing military drills the following spring. In the eyes of the Native Americans, the English were just taking advantage of them, and were getting ready to start fighting! Can you understand why they were so worried?

The local Paspahegh tribe starts causing trouble for the colonists, and the colonists do the same to them. They even get to the point of kidnapping members of each other's group. When the winter comes that year, and the colonists once again start to get very hungry (and once again don't have any of their own food) they try to go to their neighbors to buy some corn; but, as you can imagine, none of the native Americans are too eager to help them. In fact, many of the local Paspahegh people had left their villages and moved away. The few who stay were forced- at the end of a gun- to sell what they had to the colonists.

By early 1609, Captain John Smith was acting as president of the Jamestown Colony. During one battle with the local Native Americans, he captured the *weroance* (local chief) of the Paspahegh, named Wowinchapuncke, and held him captive. Although he later escaped, this helped the two groups to make some kind of peace agreement (a truce). However, listen to Wowinchapuncke's words, because they tell us what many Native American's at the time were thinking:

"We perceive and well knowe you intend to destroy us, that are here to intreat and desire your friendship..."

Were you able to understand what the chief told John Smith? In other words, he said: 'Although we are here, just trying to be your friends, deep down we can see and we know that you just plan on killing all of us anyway.' What do you think? Was the Chief right, or was he just exaggerating? Let's find out what happened later, and we will learn the answer.

In October of 1609, Captain John Smith returned to England. The man left in charge, George Percy, wasn't as good as a leader as Smith had been, and wasn't able to negotiate help and supplies from the Native Americans like Smith had done either. In fact, when he was president, during the winter of 1609-1610, Jamestown passed a period known as "the Starving Time". Why do you think they called it that? Over 80% of the colonists died that winter. Can you imagine? 80%, that's eight out of every ten people, died because they didn't have enough food. Think about the kids you go to school with. Can you imagine eight out of every ten of them dying?

The President or Jamestown, George Percy, described it like this:

"Now all of us at James Town [began] to feel that sharp prick of hunger, which no man truly describe but he which hath tasted the bitterness thereof."

Things were tough. By May of 1610, the colonists plan on leaving with Thomas Gates, who had tried to arrive sooner with supplies but who had gotten lost.

On their way back to England, they are traveling down the river and who do they see but another supply ship, led by their new governor, Lord De la Warr, from London.

This new man was unlike both Smith and Percy in how he dealt with the Native Americans. Instead of peacefully negotiating, he used his military background to try to force the Native Americans to help them.

In July, he told the Paramount Chief that they must return all English property and prisoners...or else. When he didn't get the answer he wanted (the Paramount Chief told them that they needed to just stay in their fort or go home), De la Warr got hold of a Paspahegh prisoner, cut off his hand, and sent him back to the chief with a message: 'Give me what I want or I will destroy your villages'.

Wow. This man was very different from John Smith. How do you think the Chief Powhatan should have responded? Was Lord De la Warr being fair and reasonable, or was he acting like a schoolyard bully? What would you have done if you were the Paramount Chief?

Well, as it was, the Paramount chief did not answer him.

In August, former Governor Percy was sent with 70 men to attack the Paspahegh capital. They burned down houses, cut down crops, and even took one of the chief's wives and her children. They threw her children into the water and shot them in their heads, and then they stabbed the wife herself in Jamestown. The Paspahegh, after that vicious attack, abandoned their village.

This act was like a match that lit the fuse of a war, a war that would come to be called the First Anglo-Powhatan War (the first of three, unfortunately). The colonists and the Native Americans began to fight constantly, especially in what are called "skirmishes", or, unplanned battles. The chief of the Paspahegh was killed in February 1611 in one of these battles. Although his people got some kind of revenge against a few English soldiers, the Paspahegh tribe never really recovered from all of the attacks. They merged with other tribes. Thus, the Paspahegh tribe, the first ones to make contact with the colonists when they arrived in Jamestown and to welcome them with open arms ceased to exist as a people.

What do you think about that?

The fighting continued, and in early 1613, Pocahontas herself was captured by the English. In March of 1614, she was used as leverage to make peace with the Chief Powhatan, and relations between the Native

Americans and the colonists were better after that for almost a decade.

There were two more "Anglo-Powhatan" wars after this one (including one terrible massacre by Native Americans in 1622).

When a treaty after the third war was signed in 1646, both groups finally had a nice period of peace that lasted all the way until Bacon's Rebellion in 1676 (we'll talk about that in a little bit).

The problems with the Native Americans had finally been more or less resolved, but what a price they had to pay. There was so much death and so much suffering. Why do you think that these two groups fought so much? Do you think that they could have resolved their problems by talking more, by being more respectful? Should the English have just stayed on their little fort and not tried to colonize the whole continent? What could have prevented these wars?

Well, as it was, the conflicts with Native Americans weren't the only difficulties that the Jamestown colonists had.

Problem #2: Problems With Leadership

When the one hundred or so colonists arrived at Jamestown in 1607, about half of them weren't prepared for hard work. They had come to open up business and to be aristocratic. The other half was ready to work, but it wouldn't be fair to expect them to do double the work. In fact, even the men who were ready to work didn't know anything about farming or hunting. They knew how to build and how to make tools, but what's the point of that if you have no food? After the first tough winter, a new leader was chosen- Captain John Smith.

In January of 1608, about 100 more colonists arrived. However, the village was accidentally set on fire, and the river completely froze over. As a result the men had to live in the burnt out buildings that were left. Even though the local tribes brought some food, things were tough. Smith later said that about half of the men died that winter.

During the next year, another 150 colonists joined the group at Jamestown. Captain John Smith helped to whip the colonists into shape. If any of them thought that they were going to get a free ride in the New World, they were sorely mistaken. Quoting the Bible, a book that a lot of the men at the time respected, John Smith said: "he who works not, eats not". This was important, because it helped everyone see the importance of pulling together as a team and working together. In the New World, things would be different, not like in London where some people were born rich and never had to work a day in their lives. In Jamestown, everyone had to pitch in and help.

After Smith left, leadership changed hands several times, especially during times of conflict with Native Americans.

Meanwhile, colonists such as John Rolfe (the man who would eventually become the husband of Pocahontas) began to successfully farm tobacco, which was very good news for the London Company (remember, they are still waiting to see some profit from this trip).

In 1624, King James of England decided that Virginia should no longer be a business investment, but that it should be a royal colony. With his official power, he cancels the contract that the London Company had and appointed a governor over the new territory.

Some years later, when a man named William Berkeley was acting as governor, a large scale rebellion broke out in Virginia. Member of the community (about a thousand of them) felt that he wasn't being hard enough on the Native Americans. Led by a 29 years old farmer named Francis Bacon, they ended up attacking local Native American tribes, burning the capitol building, and looting the governor's home. It was a sad time in Jamestown. Peace was finally restored after Bacon died from an unrelated illness. About six months later, life began to return to normal.

These crises of leadership didn't help the colonists with their primary objective: to survive. More often than not, they just made life more difficult and led to setbacks. Think of all the time lost fixing the damage done by this unnecessary rebellion, and of all the tears cried unnecessarily. What do you think? Should they have been fighting to so much about who was in charge, or should they have just focused on making a living for themselves and for their families?

Chapter 4: What was It Like to be a Kid in Jamestown?

If you ever look at a list of the original Jamestown colonists, five of them list their job as "boy". What does that tell you? It tells us that there were at least some teenagers and younger children in the original colony. What do you think it would have been like to be a kid in Jamestown, especially during the early years? Do you think that you could have done it? Let's look at some of the unique challenges that we have mentioned, but this time from the perspective of a kid.

First off, there was the lack of food. What is the longest that you have ever gone without eating something? Of course, all of us go the whole night without eating anything when we sleep, but we are talking when we are awake. Have you ever gone an entire day without eating? Two days? Three days? What happens when you can only eat a little bit of food every day? Do you think that you would get scared?

Most of the adult men got very scared, and some of them even ran away from Jamestown to live with the nearby Native Americans. Would you have done the same? What about those difficult winter, where up to half of the men died. Would you have been willing to work harder the following year so as to avoid going hungry again? Would you have wanted to return to England with Thomas Gate? What would you have thought when John Smith said: "he who works not, eats not"?

These are all some very interesting questions, right? When we put ourselves in other people's shoes, sometimes we can see that they were just like us. They lived in some difficult times and had to make some tough choices.

Now, let's talk about the wars. Do you remember how one English boy was brought back to Jamestown when he got lost in the forest? Do you remember who brought him back? That's right; it was the local Native American tribe, the Paspahegh. What do you think that boy was thinking when he saw these strong Native Americans, armed with weapons, coming towards him when he was in the forest? We might think that he was afraid, but somehow they let him know that they weren't going to hurt him, and that everything would be okay. He had probably been scared from being lost, and then even more scared when he saw the Paspahegh; but how do you think he felt when they brought him back to Jamestown? Do you think that he became friends with the Native Americans who helped him?

Later on, the people of Jamestown began to fight battle after battle with the Paspahegh people and with the rest of the Powhatan Confederacy. How did this boy feel about fighting against the very same people who had helped him? Do you remember what Lord De la Warr did with a Paspahegh prisoner that he had captive? He cut off his hand and sent the man, bleeding from his arm, with no medical attention, back to the Paramount Chief with a message. As a kid, would you have thought that Lord De la Warr was being fair, or that he was being too mean to the Native Americans who had helped the colonists so much?

Finally, when Lord De la Warr kidnapped the Paspahegh Chief's wife and children, and killed them in cold blood in front of you, would you have cheered? Would you have helped to kill them? Or would you have tried to stop the ones who were doing it? Would you have been too scared to say anything?

It was not easy to be a kid back then. Most of us have seen actors pretend to die in a movie or on TV, but it's not the same as seeing a person die in real life, right in front of you. It would be especially hard if the person is a child, maybe your same age. It would also be hard of that person was your friend, or a family member.

Being a kid in Jamestown wasn't easy, because they were expected to things that adults normally do: like work hard, fight wars, and bury the dead. While they tried to make the right decisions and support the good guys, it wasn't always easy to know who was right and who was wrong.

Chapter 5: How Did the Jamestown Settlement End?

As we have seen, Jamestown was a very important place. It was the first permanent English settlement in the New World, and it helped the colonists to see how hard it would be to establish themselves in America. But what finally happened to this settlement?

As we mentioned, England eventually took control of the colony, because they thought it would become an important part of their future colonization plans. And they were right. The Virginia colony eventually was one of the thirteen colonies that gave so much money and so many goods to England.

After the capitol was burned down during the Bacon Rebellion in 1676, it had to be rebuilt. However, about thirty years later, in 1698, the capitol building was burned to the ground yet again, this time because of an accident. It was decided to rebuild it in a nearby town which would eventually be called Williamsburg.

When the government left Jamestown, many of the people did too. Within a few decades, there was no one left but a few farmers.

The area around Jamestown, although it was no longer used as a center of government, was still important in fighting some big wars later on, like the American Revolutionary War and the American Civil War (we'll learn a little more about these in the next section).

What happened after the Jamestown settlement ended?

The people who survived those first few years of the Jamestown settlement became stronger as a result of it. Captain John Smith returned to America a few years later and explored the northern region. It was him who gave it the name "New England", a name that we still use today to describe the Northeastern states.

Pocahontas eventually married a Jamestown settler and was brought to England as part of a publicity tour. While there, she got very sick and died.

Lord De la Warr returned to England in 1611. A few years later, he got on a boat to return to Virginia to address some problems there (he was still the governor) but died before the ship arrived.

George Percy returned to England and fought in some wars with England enemies. It is not known exactly when or where he died.

After the capital building was moved to nearby Williamsburg, the area of Jamestown came under private ownership. It was used by local families for agriculture (mainly by the Travis and Ambler families of Virginia). However, there were some battles fought there during two major wars in American History.

THE AMERICAN REVOLUTIONARY WAR-
THE BATTLE OF GREEN SPRING:

Basically, this was a small battle where one American Brigadier General ("Mad" Anthony Wayne) decided to attack the forces of British Earl Charles Cornwallis while these crossed the James River. Relying on some information received from "British defectors" (who were actually sent as spies with false info) the Americans decided to attack, almost fell completely into the trap. Another American Army officer, named Marquis de Lafayette, was able to help Wayne, who fought hard with bayonets. At the end of the day, 28 American soldiers had died, and 122 had been wounded (out of 800-900) while a total of 75 British soldiers were killed/wounded.

In the year 1831, a man named David Bullock purchased Jamestown from Travis and Ambler families. About thirty years later, during the American Civil War, the land once again became the location of some bloody fighting, this time between Confederate (Southern) Troop and Union (Northern) troops.

The Confederates had chosen the Jamestown area in order to block the union ship from sailing up the river and attacking the city of Richmond. In that same area, the Confederates were also experimenting with building iron clad ships (precursors to today's submarines) and they didn't want that technology to fall into the wrong hands.

On May 5, 1862, the armies of both sides met and fought a bloody battle, with 2,283 Union soldiers and 1,682 Confederate soldiers dying that day. The iron clad ship was sunk on purpose, and all the Confederate troops retreated to Richmond, a safer and more defendable position.

The area that used to be Jamestown now only had the old Ambler house and part of the old church. It became a sort of haven (a safe place) for runaway slaves. They would leave the South and then, on their way to the free North, could stay at Jamestown and receive help. In fact, when the confederate General who had fought there previously (General William Allen) came back to inspect everything a few months after the battle, he was actually killed by some of the freed slaves.

A couple named Mr. and Mrs. Edward Barney bought the land in 1892, long after the fierce fighting had ended. They donated some of the land, including the remains of the church, to a group who was dedicated to preserving the history of Virginia. This group was able to make arrangements to build a large wall to keep the sea from eroding more land from the Jamestown peninsula. They felt that future generations should know about the hard work of the original colonists, and they were sad that the foundations of the original fort had all been washed to sea. They wanted to prevent any further loss to the land. In 1936, the area was designated by the U.S. Government as a Federal Park, called the Colonial National Historical Park.

Something very interesting happened in 1996. Do you remember how everyone thought that the original fort had been washed to sea? In 1996, a project (called the Jamestown Rediscovery Project) discovered that only a small part of the original fort had been washed out to sea. In reality, the sea wall had preserved the original fort. Since then, hundreds or thousands of artifacts, including graves, have been found. Some buildings have even been partially reconstructed using the information they have found.

Conclusion

What are some of the lessons that can be learned for the Jamestown settlement? Because this was the first settlement in American history, it really set the tone for how things would be done for the following decades and centuries. Let's look at three areas where the colonists had difficulties, to see what they learned (and how things have been ever since):

1) The need for good leaders

2) The need to work together

3) The need to respect foreign nations

The Need for Good Leaders

Do you remember how tough things were when the colonists did not have a leader with the necessary qualities? For example, when George Percy was in charge, the people had a really tough time. Over 80% of the colonists died during one winter, a period they called "the Starving Time". Part of the problem was that he didn't know how to negotiate with the Native Americans like John Smith had done. Later on, Lord De la Warr was so harsh with the Native Americans that he ended up starting a war with them, a war which led to the death and suffering of many people.

What do you think it would have been like if the Jamestown colony had had different leaders? For example, if George Percy had been a better negotiator, would less people have died? If Lord De la Warr had not been so violent, would less people have died?

The lessons learned were clear: the success of the early colonists, and of all future Americans, would depend on their finding good leaders. What do you think: have Americans been successful since then at choosing good leaders? Have they learned their lesson about not choosing men who are too violent or who have no people skills?

The Need to Work Together

The early colonists also learned that a society cannot function if only some people work while others just sit back and relax. Do you remember what John Smith said when some of the Jamestown colonists refused to work? He said "that he that will not work shall not eat…" The colonists had to learn to work together and to help each other if they were to survive.

What do you think? Have the American people learned this lesson? Have they learned about how important it is for everyone to work hard, and that everyone must learn to work together? When you look at the United States today, do you see anyone who is like one of the original Jamestown colonists, a little lazy, wanting everyone else to do the hard work while they stay home and relax? What about you? Are you willing to work hard?

The Need to Respect Foreign Nations

Another very important lesson that the Jamestown colonists had to learn had to do with getting along with foreign nations, in this case, the Powhatan Native Americans. From the very beginning, the Jamestown colonists had disagreements with, disrespected, and eventually fought with and killed the Native Americans. Of course, the Native Americans themselves were not completely innocent, as they also fought with, argued with, and killed the colonists. But what do you think? Did it have to be that way? Did all of those people have to die?

These aren't easy questions. None of us were there, so we can't be one hundred sure of what they were thinking. But do you think it would've helped the colonists to put themselves in the place of the Native Americans and see things from their point of view?

For example, let's say that you are an average member of the Paspahegh tribe in Eastern Virginia. One day, you see these strange looking men arrive unannounced on your land. Of course, you invite these men as guests, you give them food, and you want them to be comfortable. But then, they begin to build a house- on your land. They begin to steal food-from your family members. They pick fights- with your friends. They start practicing their military skills and getting ready for a fight. Would you be afraid?

The colonists were just trying to survive, but they felt that they were entitled to take this new land. Do you think they could have lived in Jamestown more peaceably if they had tried to build better relations with this foreign nation? Could they have avoided the many wars and deaths that followed?

Have Americans learned any lessons since then? Do you think that they have learned to live in peace with other nations, understanding their differences and trying to help each other? Or do you think that Americans are like the early colonists, only worried about themselves, and often acting out of fear?

Like before, these aren't easy questions to answer. We can't always know what people were thinking. Even today, we can't read other people's minds. But don't you think it's worth trying, if it means we can avoid big wars and lots of death?

If you visit Easter Virginia today, you can visit the towns of Williamsburg, and see the archeologists digging at Jamestown. You can see three huge ships, built just like the three original ships that brought the colonists to Jamestown. You can see actors dressed up in period clothes, and visit a recreation of a Native American village. You can work on the ships, try on colonial armor, and even try some of the food! You

can see what it was like to live back then!

Being a colonist in Jamestown wasn't easy. It required hard work and quick thinking. A lot of people suffered, but they laid the foundation for the country that we know today as the United States. In this handbook, we learned about their challenges, and about some of the decisions that they made. Of course, not all of their decisions were the right ones, but it was hard to know that at the time.

Have you learned anything after reading about the Jamestown colonists? Will you try to learn from their mistakes, and do the same good things that they did? If so, you too can be a success story that people might talk about in the future!

Cover Image © styf - Fotolia.com.jpg

Made in the USA
Middletown, DE
12 October 2015